# Nasreddin Hodja

*Story Cards*

*Stories to Read and Retell*

*Compiled by Raymond C. Clark*

*Illustrations by Robert MacLean*

**Pro Lingua Associates, Publishers**
74 Cotton Mill Hill, Suite A315
Brattleboro, Vermont 05301 USA
Office: 802 257 7779
Orders: 800 366 4775
www.ProLinguaAssociates.com
Fax: 802 257 5117
E-mail: orders@ProLinguaAssociates.com
SAN: 216-0579

*At Pro Lingua*
*our objective is to foster an approach*
*to learning and teaching that we call*
**interplay**, *the* **inter***action of language*
*learners and teachers with their materials,*
*with the language and culture,*
*and with each other in active, creative*
*and productive* **play**.

Third, revised edition copyright © 2017 by Raymond C. Clark
This third edition is in Story Card format, as was the first edition © 1991.
Nasreddin Hodja is also available in an interactive digital edition © 2017.
An expanded audio CD with twenty-six additional Hodja stories for
listening practice is available at www.ProLinguaAssociates.com.

ISBN 978-0-86647-441-2

Digital edition ISBN 978-0-86647-405-4  Audio CD ISBN 13: 978-0-86647-215-9

These Story Cards were designed by Arthur A. Burrows and set in Palatino;
They were printed by King Printing Company in Lowell, Massachusetts.

Illustrations by Robert MacLean

Printed in the United States of America
Third Edition 2017

There was a man who often asked Hodja for advice. Usually Hodja thought the man's problems were not very important. One day he came to Hodja with this problem: "I have a headache. What should I do?"

Hodja replied, "I'm not sure, my friend, but I can tell you that recently I had a toothache. I had the tooth pulled out, and it doesn't bother me now."

# 1
## *The Cure for a Headache*

man

advice

important

problem

headache

recently

toothache

pulled out

bother

Hodja was once the preacher in his town. He often argued with the mayor, who always disagreed with him. One day the mayor died, and the people came to Hodja. They asked him to say a prayer for the dead mayor.

"No, it's no use," said Hodja. "He never listened to me when he was alive."

# 2
## *A Frightening Place*

visitor
question
place
come from
frightening
why
come
babies
crying
go
everybody

One day a visitor came to Hodja with a
question. "Hodja, the place that we humans
come from and the place that we go to,
what is it like?"

"Oh," said Hodja, "it is a very frightening place."

"Why do you say that?" the visitor asked.

"Well, when we come from there as babies, we
are crying, and when somebody has to go there,
everybody cries."

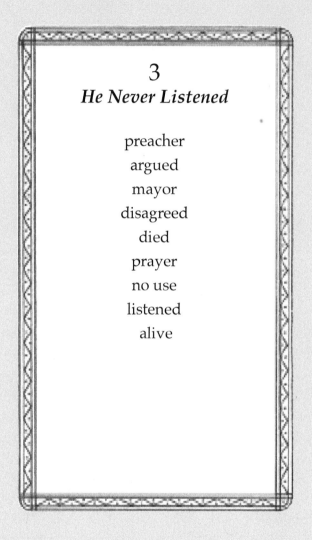

# 3
## *He Never Listened*

preacher
argued
mayor
disagreed
died
prayer
no use
listened
alive

The hair on a man's head often turns grey before his beard. As Hodja became older, his hair turned white, but his beard didn't.

At the barber shop one day, one of his friends said to Hodja, "Hodja, your hair is almost white, but your beard is still black as coal. Why is that?"

Hodja answered, "Why, that's easy to explain. The hair on my head is twenty years older than my beard."

# 4
## Hodja's Hair

hair
gray
beard
older
white
barber shop
beard
still black
explain
head
older
beard

Nasreddin Hodja was walking down the street one day when he noticed something shining in the dirt. He walked over and picked it up. It was a small mirror. He looked in it, saw himself, and then threw it away, saying to his neighbor who was watching him, "It is not surprising, my friend, that someone threw that thing away. Who would want to keep such an ugly picture?"

# 5
## *An Ugly Picture*

walking

street

noticed

shining

dirt

picked up

mirror

threw away

neighbor

watching

keep

ugly

Hodja often took donkeys to the market to sell, and he sold his donkeys for a very low price. One day another donkey seller said to him, "How can you sell your donkeys so cheaply? I cannot do it, although I pay my servants almost nothing, and I have my servants steal the hay from the fields."

"Well," said Hodja, "it's easy to explain. You steal hay and labor; I steal donkeys."

# 6
## *Cheap Donkeys*

donkeys
market
low price
seller
cheap
pay
servants
steal
hay
explain
labor
hay
donkeys

Hodja's neighbor built a new house, and when he finished, a big pile of dirt remained. Weeks went by, and Hodja got tired of looking out his window at the dirt pile. So one day he got out his shovel, and beside his neighbor's dirt pile, he began to dig a hole.

His neighbor came out and asked, "Hodja, what are you doing that for?"

Hodja replied, "My friend, I'm going to bury your pile of dirt."

# 7
## *A Pile of Dirt*

neighbor

new house

pile

dirt

tired

shovel

dig

hole

what . . . for

replied

bury

Once Hodja was seriously ill, and he lay in his bed at home. His wife was very concerned and came to his bed crying.

When Hodja saw her crying he said to her, "Why are you crying, my dear? Go put on your best clothes and smile."

"But why?" she asked. "Hodja, I can't do that, not while you're in pain!"

Hodja smiled at her and said, "My dear, I want you to do it. If the angel of death comes, he will see how beautiful you are and take you instead."

# 8
## *The Angel of Death*

ill
bed
wife
crying
best clothes
smile
why
pain
angel
death
beautiful
instead

One day Hodja walked into a tea shop and sat down beside a friend.

"How are you?" asked the friend.

"Well, to tell the truth," said Hodja, "I'm a little thirsty and hungry. I haven't been able to drink or eat a thing for the past three days."

"My dear Hodja," said the friend, "let me buy you some tea and pastries," and he ordered some. "You must have been quite ill," the friend said, "What was wrong?"

"Oh, I wasn't ill," said Hodja. "I was broke."

# 9
## *Nothing to Eat*

tea shop

friend

thirsty

hungry

three days

buy

pastries

quite ill

wrong

broke

One day Hodja told his son to get the water pot and go to the well for some water. He told him, "Be careful, son, and do not break the pot." Then, just as the boy was about to go, Hodja put him over his knee and spanked him.

"What did you do that for?" asked a neighbor. "He didn't do anything wrong."

"Not yet," said Hodja, "but if he breaks the pot, then it will be too late to punish him."

# 10
## *Don't Break the Pot*

son

water pot

well

careful

break

about to

knee

spank

wrong

not yet

break

too late

punish

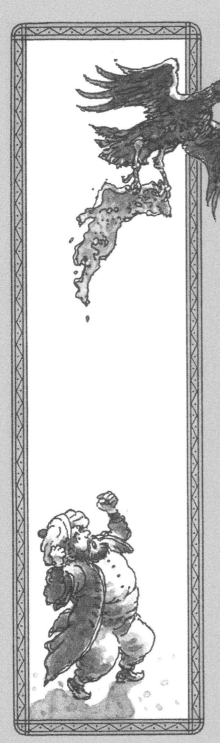

One day Hodja went to the market and bought a fine piece of meat. On the way home he met a friend who gave him a special recipe for the meat. Hodja was very happy. But then, before he got home, a large crow stole the meat from Hodja's hands and flew off with it.

"You thief!" Hodja angrily called after the departing crow. "You have stolen my meat! But you won't enjoy it; I've got the recipe!"

# 11
## *The Stolen Meat*

market
bought
meat
friend
recipe
crow
flew off
thief
stolen
enjoy
recipe

One day a friend came to Hodja's house to borrow a donkey.

"I'm sorry," said Hodja, "but I've already lent it to somebody else."

Just then the donkey made a loud noise from the back of the house.

"Hodja," the man said, "I just heard your donkey! It's out back."

Angrily, Hodja asked his friend to leave the house. "What kind of friend are you?" he said. "You believe my donkey but you don't believe me!"

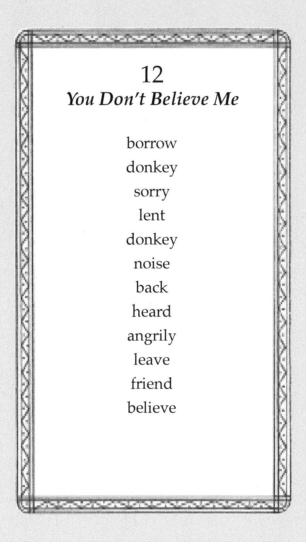

## 12
## *You Don't Believe Me*

borrow

donkey

sorry

lent

donkey

noise

back

heard

angrily

leave

friend

believe

A group of religious leaders got into an argument during a meeting. Half of the group insisted that it was proper to walk on the *left* side of a coffin as it was being carried to the cemetery. The other half claimed that the *right* side was proper.

They couldn't reach an agreement, so they decided to consult Hodja.

Hodja thought about this matter for a moment, and then he said, "My friends, left side or right side of the coffin doesn't really matter. What matters is outside or inside."

# 13
## *Which Side of the Coffin?*

religious leaders

argument

proper

left

coffin

cemetery

right

consult

thought

matter

outside

inside

odja went to the bazaar one day to buy some trousers. He picked out a pair, and the shopkeeper wrapped them up. Just then Hodja saw a coat that he liked better.

"Give me the coat instead," said Hodja.

The shopkeeper then wrapped up the coat and gave it to Hodja. Hodja was about to walk away when the shopkeeper said, "Wait, Hodja! You didn't pay for the coat!"

"But I left you the trousers," said Hodja.

"But you didn't pay for the trousers."

"Of course not! Why should I pay for something I didn't buy?"

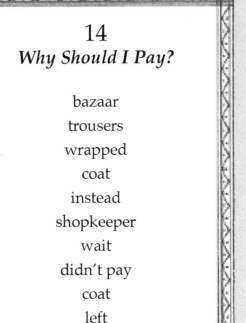

# 14
## *Why Should I Pay?*

bazaar

trousers

wrapped

coat

instead

shopkeeper

wait

didn't pay

coat

left

trousers

didn't pay

didn't buy

Hodja bought a large sack of potatoes at the market. He put the sack over his shoulder, got on his donkey, and started to ride home. On the way, he met a friend who said, "Hodja, isn't it difficult to hold the sack with one hand and guide your donkey with the other? Why don't you just tie the sack to the donkey?"

"Oh, friend," said Hodja, "my poor donkey has a heavy load just carrying me, so I am happy to carry the sack myself."

# 15
## *The Sack of Potatoes*

sack

potatoes

shoulder

donkey

friend

difficult

hold

guide

tie

donkey

load

carry

myself

It was a hot day and Hodja was tired from walking. So he sat down under the shade of a large walnut tree which was next to a garden full of watermelons. As he sat there, he began thinking to himself.

"It is strange," he thought, "that Allah should have these large watermelons grow on such small plants, whereas the little walnut grows on such a large tree."

Just then, a walnut fell from the tree and hit Hodja on the head. "Ah," thought Hodja. "Allah knows what he's doing."

# 16
## *Allah Knows*
## *What He's Doing*

walking

shade

walnut

watermelons

thinking

strange

God

small plants

large tree

fell

head

knows

In the old days it was possible for a man to have more than one wife. Hodja also married a second time. His new wife was younger than the first one.

One evening Hodja came home to find them quarreling. They were arguing about which of them Hodja loved more. At first, Hodja said that he loved them both, but they weren't satisfied.

The older one said, "Suppose the three of us were in a boat and it started to sink. Which one of us would you try to save?"

Hodja thought for a moment, and then said to his older wife. "My dear, you know how to swim, don't you?"

# 17
## *The Sinking Boat*

old days

wife

second

younger

quarelling

which

suppose

boat

sink

save

older

swim

Nasreddin Hodja was an educated, literate man, and one day an illiterate farmer came to him and asked him to write a letter for him.

"Where will you send it?" asked Hodja.

"To Baghdad," replied the farmer.

"Oh, but I can't possibly go there," said Hodja.

The farmer was a little puzzled, and so he said, "I don't want you to go there. I want to send a letter there."

"Ah yes," said Hodja. "But you see, my handwriting is so bad that nobody can read it, so I'll have to go there and read the letter to them."

# 18
## *The Letter to Baghdad*

educated

literate

illiterate

write

where

Baghdad

go

puzzled

send

handwriting

nobody

read

Hodja was up working on his roof one day when a stranger came to the house and knocked on the door. Hodja looked down at him and said, "What do you want?"

"Come down and I'll tell you," said the stranger. So Hodja climbed slowly down the ladder. When he was on the ground, the man said, "Please, would you give me some money?"

Hodja looked at him and said, "Come up on the roof with me."

The man followed Hodja slowly up the ladder, and when he got to the roof, Hodja turned to him and said, "No."

# 19
## *Come up on the Roof*

working

roof

stranger

knocked

looked down

come down

climbed

ladder

money

come up

followed

roof

no

---

One day Hodja went to visit a neighbor. When Hodja knocked on the door, the neighbor stuck his head out of the upstairs window. When he saw Hodja, he quickly pulled it back again, because he did not want to see him. The neighbor told his wife, "Go downstairs and tell Hodja that I am not here."

So the wife went down and told Hodja that her husband had gone out.

"All right," said Hodja, "but please tell him when he goes out he should take his head with him.

# 20
## *The Neighbor's Head*

visit

knocked

stuck

head

upstairs window

pulled back

told

wife

not here

husband

goes out

head

Hodja was once a judge. One day a man came to his house to complain about his neighbor. Hodja listened carefully and then said to him, "My good man, you are right." The man went away happy.

In a little while the first man's neighbor came to see Hodja. He complained about the first man. Hodja listened carefully to him, too, and then said, "My good man, you are right."

Hodja's wife had been listening to all this, and when the second man left, she turned to Hodja and said, "Hodja, you told both men they were right. That's impossible. They both can't be right."

Hodja listened carefully to his wife and then said to her, "My dear, you are right."

# 21
## *Everybody's Right*

judge
complain
listened
right
neighbor
complained
right
wife
both
impossible
carefully
right

When Hodja's wife died, he was heartbroken and he mourned for days. His friends tried to comfort him. One of them said, "Hodja, please don't worry, my friend. We'll find a new wife for you."

Sometime later, Hodja's donkey died and he seemed to be even more unhappy. Again everyone tried to comfort him, but it did no good. His sadness only increased. Finally, one of them said, "Hodja, why are you so sad?"

Hodja responded to him like this: "My friend, when my wife died, everyone promised to find another wife for me, but now that my donkey has died, nobody has offered to get me another donkey."

## 22
### The Dead Donkey

wife
died
heartbroken
mourned
comfort
find
new wife
donkey
unhappy
sadness
promised
nobody
offered
donkey

For a while Hodja served as advisor to the king.

One day the king's chef prepared a very tasty dish of egg plant and other vegetables. As Hodja and the king were eating, the king said to Hodja, "Isn't this dish the best you have ever eaten?"

"Oh yes, majesty, the very best," said Hodja.

"Then I want it served every day," said the king. But after ten more meals the king turned to Hodja and said, "Take this away. This food is terrible."

"Yes indeed it is," Hodja agreed.

"But Hodja," said the king, "just a few days ago you said this was a wonderful dish."

"Oh, I did, your majesty, but I serve you, not the vegetables."

# 23
## *The Wonderful Vegetable Dish*

served

advisor

chef

eggplant

best

every day

ten meals

terrible

yes, indeed

but

wonderful

serve

vegetables

Hodja and some friends were discussing food one day. One of the men asked Hodja which food he liked best.

Hodja replied that he liked helva, a dessert that is made of flour, butter, and sugar.

"But unfortunately, we never have it at our house," said Hodja.

His friends asked him why, and he replied, "Well, when we have flour, there is no sugar. When there is sugar, we have no butter. When there is butter, there is no flour."

"But certainly," said one of the men, "at some time all of the ingredients must be available at the same time."

"Yes," said Hodja, "that's true. There was a time when we had everything, but unfortunately, I wasn't at home then."

# 24
## *No Helva at Home*

discussing
food
helva
unfortunately
why
flour
sugar
butter
all ingredients
available
unfortunately
at home

Hodja and his wife sometimes quarreled, like any married couple. One night they got into a fierce quarrel.

The next day when Hodja left the house he seemed to be very angry.

"What happened last night?" a neighbor asked.

"Oh, my wife and I just had a little argument," said Hodja.

"Yes, we heard you, but what was that loud noise at the end of the quarrel?"

"Oh that," said Hodja. "My wife was so angry she threw my coat down the stairs."

The neighbor was puzzled. "But a coat wouldn't make so much noise."

Said Hodja, "It did, my friend, because I was in it."

# 25
## *The Noisy Coat*

quarreled

fierce

next day

angry

neighbor

argument

loud noise

coat

stairs

puzzled

because

A group of soldiers came to the village tea shop and began to talk about their battles and success in war. The villagers listened eagerly as the soldiers described how they fought and chased away the enemy.

Hodja, who had never really been a great soldier, wanted to get some of the attention.

"That reminds me of the time," said Hodja, "when with one swing of my great sword I cut off the leg of an enemy soldier."

One of the soldiers then turned to Hodja and said, "It would have been better to cut off his head."

"Of course!" said Hodja, "but somebody else had already done that."

51

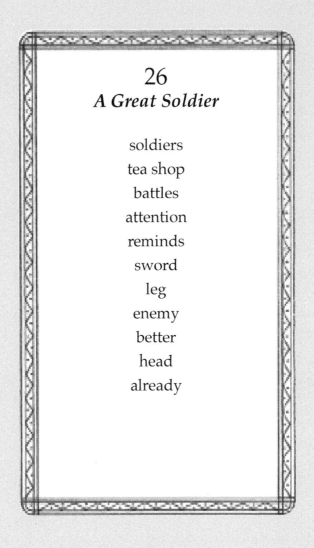

# 26
## *A Great Soldier*

soldiers

tea shop

battles

attention

reminds

sword

leg

enemy

better

head

already

One day a friend came to Hodja to ask him for a loan. Hodja did not really trust the man, and he expected that he would never be repaid. Nevertheless, he was a friend, so Hodja loaned him the money.

Hodja was surprised when a few days later the man came back and repaid the loan in full.

A month or so later, the friend came back for another loan and said to him, "You know my credit is good, Hodja. I repaid my last loan in just a few days."

But Hodja said to him, "You deceived me before. You repaid the loan and I thought you wouldn't. But you won't deceive me again because this time I won't give you a loan."

## 27
### *No Loan for You*

friend
loan
trust
repaid
nevertheless
surprised
later
came back
another loan
credit
deceived
before
won't deceive
loan

Hodja's wife was very angry with him one day, so she decided to play a trick on him. She prepared a soup for the evening dinner and put a lot of hot pepper in it.

Just before serving the soup, she decided to taste it. That was a mistake. Even a small spoonful was so hot it brought tears to her eyes.

As she served Hodja the soup, he noticed her tears and asked her why she was crying.

"I am crying because my poor, dear mother is dead and gone!" said Hodja's wife.

Then Hodja took a spoonful, and tears came to his eyes also. His wife, trying to hide her pleasure, asked him, "And, husband, why are you crying?"

Hodja replied, "I am crying because your poor, dear mother is dead and gone, and you are alive and here."

# 28
## *Pepper Soup*

wife
angry
trick
soup
pepper
taste
tears
noticed
why
mother
dead and gone
tears
why
mother
you
alive and here

A stranger came up to Hodja and asked him to change a gold coin. Actually, Hodja did not have any money, but he didn't want to admit it, so he took the coin and studied it carefully. Then he handed the coin back to the man saying, "I'm sorry, my friend, but this coin is underweight. I can't give you its face value."

"That's all right, just give me what it's worth," said the stranger.

"Oh, but it's very underweight," said Hodja.

"But, Hodja, I need the change right away. Just give me whatever it's worth."

Hodja looked again at the coin and then said, "My friend, this coin is so underweight, that if I change it, you will owe me money."

# 29
## *The Underweight Coin*

change
gold coin
didn't have
studied
underweight
face value
all right
very underweight
whatever
worth
so underweight
owe

One day Hodja went to the Turkish bath. He was poorly dressed, and the attendants gave him only a small piece of soap, a dirty, torn towel, and very poor service.

When he had finished, he tipped each of the attendants a nice gold coin as he went out the door.

A few days later Hodja came back again, only this time he was dressed in his finest clothes. Of course, the attendants treated him much better, expecting an even better tip.

As he went out the door, he gave each of them a worthless copper coin.

"Hodja," one of them said, "we treated you very well. Why do you tip so poorly?"

Hodja smiled and said. "The copper coins are for the first time I came. The gold coins were for this time."

# 30
## *An Even Better Tip*

Turkish bath

poorly dressed

soap

towel

poor service

tipped

gold coin

came back

finest clothes

expecting

copper coin

why

first time

this time

One day Hodja came back from the market with a very nice piece of meat for dinner. He left it with his wife and went out to have a cup of tea.

While he was gone, his wife prepared a wonderful shish kebab, but it looked and smelled so good she couldn't resist tasting it. Just then, some of her friends came by, and in a short time the meat was all gone.

Hodja returned for dinner, but his wife served him a thin, watery soup instead of the meat.

"But where is the meat?" asked Hodja.

"Oh, the cat ate it," said his wife.

"But it was a whole kilo," said Hodja. He then found the cat and put it on the scales. It weighed one kilo.

"So, I have found the meat," Hodja said. "Now, where is the cat?"

# 31
## The Cat and the Meat

market

meat

left

shish kebab

friends

all gone

returned

where

cat

kilo

scales

one kilo

meat

where

cat

One day Hodja was walking quietly along the street when a troublesome villager came up behind him and slapped him on the back. Then he excused himself saying, "I'm so sorry, Hodja, I thought you were someone else – a friend of mine," and he laughed.

Angered, Hodja grabbed the man and took him to the court. At the court he asked the judge to fine the man for his offensive behavior.

"But Hodja," said the judge, "this is really quite minor. Why don't you forget it?"

However, Hodja insisted, and so the judge fined the man two small coins. The man agreed right away to pay the fine, but he told Hodja to wait a minute while he went home to get the money.

Hodja waited and waited, but the man didn't come back.

Finally, Hodja walked up to the judge and slapped him on the back saying, "There, now when he comes he can pay you the coins."

# 32
## *A Slap on the Back*

walking
troublesome
slapped
sorry
laughed
grabbed
court
judge
fine
minor
forget
insisted
two small coins
agreed
wait
money
come back
slapped
pay you

A poor hungry man was walking along the street with just a piece of bread in his hand. He came to a restaurant where he saw some meatballs being grilled. The cooking meat was so near and the smell was so delicious. The man held his piece of bread over the meat to catch some of its wonderful smell. As he started to eat the bread, the angry restaurant owner seized him and took him away to see the judge, who happened to be Hodja.

"This man was stealing the smell of my meat without asking permission," said the restaurant owner. "I want you to make him pay me."

Hodja thought for a minute and then held his purse in front of the owner and shook it.

"What are you doing that for?" asked the owner.

Hodja replied, "I am paying you. The sound of money is fair payment for the smell of food."

# 33
## *The Sound of Money*

hungry

bread

restaurant

meatballs

smell

held

catch

owner

judge

stealing

permission

pay

purse

shook

what . . . for

sound

money

payment

One day Hodja borrowed a large pot from his neighbor. After a few days he returned it to the owner, along with a small pot.

"What is this?" asked the neighbor, pointing to the small pot.

"Oh," said Hodja, "Your big pot had a baby while it was at my house."

Naturally, the neighbor was pleased to get an extra pot so he accepted it.

A week or so later, Hodja borrowed the large pot again. But this time he didn't return it. So one day the neighbor came to Hodja's house and asked him for the pot.

"I can't give it back, because it died," said Hodja.

"You're crazy," said the neighbor. "A cooking pot can't die."

"Why not?" said Hodja. "If you believe it can give birth, why can't you believe it can die?"

67

## 34
### *The Dead Pot*

borrowed

large

returned

small

baby

pleased

accepted

borrowed

return

give back

died

crazy

believe

give birth

Hodja and a friend were returning to their village when they stopped for lunch. They spread out a few things to eat, including a pot of yogurt.

Now, this friend was well known as a very stingy person. As Hodja took out his spoon, the friend sprinkled sugar on half of the surface and told Hodja, "I like to eat yogurt with sugar on it."

"May I have some on my half?" asked Hodja.

"Oh no, I don't have much and it's expensive," said the friend.

Hodja thought for a moment, and then pulled a bottle of vinegar from his sack and started to pour it on the yogurt.

"Wait!" said his friend, "What are you doing?"

"I happen to like vinegar on my yogurt, and so I'm pouring some on my half," Hodja said, as the vinegar slowly spread across the surface of the yogurt.

# 35
## *Sugar on Yogurt*

friend

lunch

yogurt

stingy

sugar

my half

expensive

vinegar

pour

wait

what

like

vinegar

spread

surface

Hodja was invited to a big feast at the house of a very rich man. He went but he wore his usual, everyday clothes. Once he got to the banquet the guests, who were very richly dressed, and the servants all ignored him. After a while Hodja went home and put on his very best clothes, a beautiful turban, a silk robe, fine jewelry, and a magnificent fur coat.

He returned to the feast, and this time everyone welcomed him and talked to him. The host asked Hodja to sit beside him at the table. The servants came and filled his plate with delicious food.

But Hodja surprised everyone. He took off his coat and held it to the plate, saying, "Eat, my good fur coat, eat. Enjoy the meal."

His host was astonished and said to Hodja, "What are you doing?"

Hodja replied, "It is the clothes you invited to this feast, not me."

# 36
## *The Clothes and the Feast*

big feast
rich man
everyday clothes
ignored
went home
best clothes
fur coat
returned
welcomed
host
beside
surprised
held
plate
eat
astonished
what
clothes
invited

Once Hodja had a fat, young lamb which he liked very much. One day some friends were visiting, and they proposed to Hodja that they kill the lamb and have a feast. At first Hodja resisted, but finally one of them said, "Look, Hodja, the day of judgment will come to all of us soon, so why don't we enjoy life's pleasures now?"

Reluctantly, Hodja agreed, and they all went to the bank of a river. They built a fire and killed and roasted the lamb. After the feast, the other men took off their clothes and went swimming in the river.

While they were swimming, Hodja threw their clothes on the fire. His friends came back and couldn't find their clothes. Then they realized that Hodja had burned them.

"What did you do that for?" they asked.

Hodja replied, "The fire needed fuel, and see how well it is burning now to keep you warm. And since the day of judgment is coming soon, what do you need the clothes for?"

# 37
## *The Day of Judgement*

young, fat lamb
friends
visiting
kill
feast
resisted
the day of judgement
enjoy
pleasures
now
reluctantly
fire
roasted
clothes
swimming
fire
burned
what . . . for
fuel
warm
coming soon

Hodja was in the market one day when he noticed a man with a cage in his hand. There was a parrot in the cage, and the man was selling his parrot, shouting out to the market goers, "100 gold ducas!" As Hodja watched, someone bought the parrot.

Hodja suddenly saw a chance to make some money, so he rushed home and got a turkey from his back yard. He returned to the market and began shouting, "200 gold ducas for this beautiful turkey!" But nobody showed any interest.

Finally a friend came up to Hodja and said to him, "Hodja, are you crazy? You can't sell a turkey for that price!"

Hodja said, "Why not? My turkey is as beautiful as a parrot that was sold for 100 ducas this morning, and my turkey is bigger."

"But Hodja," the friend said, "that parrot is valuable because it talks like a man."

"Is that so?" said Hodja. "Well, my turkey thinks like a man."

# 38
## *The Thinking Turkey*

market

cage

parrot

100 gold ducas

bought

chance

money

home

turkey

200 gold ducas

nobody

crazy

why not

beautiful

bigger

talks

thinks

One Friday Nasreddin Hodja came to the mosque to give a sermon. He got up in the pulpit and said to the people, "Do you know what I'm going to talk about today?"

Surprised, the people said, "No, we have no idea."

"Well then," said Hodja, "there's no point in my talking to you, because you won't understand," and he went home.

The next Friday, he came again to the mosque and again said to the people, "Do you know what I'm going to talk about?"

This time the listeners were prepared, and so one of them said, "Yes, we do!"

"In that case," Hodja said, "there's no point in my talking to you because you already understand."

Then, on the next Friday, he came and asked the same question, "Do you know what I'm going to talk about?"

Now the listeners were prepared again. "Some of us do, and some don't," they said.

"All right, then," Hodja said. "Those who know what I'm going to talk about tell those who don't know," and he went home.

## 39
## *The Sermon*

mosque

sermon

pulpit

know

no idea

no point

understand

home

next Friday

this time

prepared

no point

already

next Friday

some do

those

tell

those

home

Hodja went to the bazaar to buy a donkey. He finally chose one and paid the two men who sold it to him. He didn't realize that the two men were cleaver thieves.

As Hodja was leading the donkey home, the two men came up behind him. They slipped the rope off the donkey's neck. One man put the rope on his own neck and followed behind Hodja. The other quietly led the donkey back to the bazaar to sell it again

After a while, Hodja turned around and saw the man. "What are you doing here?" he exclaimed.

The thief said, "I disobeyed my mother, and as a punishment I was turned into a donkey. But now, praise God, I have been bought by an honest man and the spell is broken."

"How wonderful!" said Hodja. "Now go back home and never disobey your mother again."

The next day Hodja went back to the bazaar, and there was the first donkey seller standing beside the donkey Hodja had bought the day before.

Amazed, Hodja walked up to the donkey and said angrily, "You fool! I thought I told you never to disobey your mother again!"

## 40
### *Obey Your Mother*

bazaar
donkey
thieves
leading
rope
own neck
followed
other
turned around
what
disobeyed
turned into
bought
honest man
spell
wonderful
never
next day
donkey
amazed
fool
disobey

# Nasreddin Hodja

*Introduction and Teachers' Guide*
*Stories to Read and Retell*

Compiled by Raymond C. Clark
Illustrations by Robert MacLean

**Pro Lingua Associates, Publishers**
74 Cotton Mill Hill, Suite A315
Brattleboro, Vermont 05301 USA
Office: 802 257 7779
Orders: 800 366 4775
www.ProLinguaAssociates.com
Fax: 802 257 5117
E-mail: orders@ProLinguaAssociates.com
SAN: 216-0579

*At Pro Lingua*
*our objective is to foster an approach*
*to learning and teaching that we call*
**interplay**, *the* **inter***action of language*
*learners and teachers with their materials,*
*with the language and culture,*
*and with each other in active, creative*
*and productive* **play***.*

Third, revised edition copyright © 2017 by Raymond C. Clark
The first edition was © 1991; the second edition © 2004.
Nasreddin Hodja is also available in an interactive digital edition © 2017.
An expanded audio CD with twenty-six additional Hodja stories for
listening practice is available at www.ProLinguaAssociates.com.

ISBN 978-0-86647-441-2
Digital edition ISBN 978-0-86647-405-4
Audio CD ISBN 13: 978-0-86647-215-9

These Story Cards were designed by Arthur A. Burrows and set in Palatino;
they were printed by King Printing Company in Lowell, Massachusetts.

Illustrations by Robert MacLean

Printed in the United States of America
Third Edition 2017

2

# Contents

# *Introduction*

This collection features the humorous folk tales attributed to Nasreddin Hodja, a Turkish legend. The stories are known throughout the world of Islam.

The first edition of Ray Clark's collection was published in 1991 in Story Card format – each illustrated tale on a separate card. In 2004 Pro Lingua brought out a new edition as a reader with pages that were easy to remove to make cards. Ray added an additional twenty-six to the book and recorded them all to provide listening practice – an audio book. In 2017 a digital edition of the first forty stories is being published with audio and interactive exercises. The audio book CD is still available, and in response to pleas from several teachers who have loved the Story Card format of the tales, this third edition is now available.

The basic idea of this collection of stories is quite simple: People like to read, tell, and listen to stories, jokes, and anecdotes. In this collection there are 40 illustrated stories, each on one page, backed by a page of prompts. Each story is a short, humorous tale in clear, modified English. The cards progress from short and easy to longer and more difficult. They can be used by a range of learners, from beginners to students at the advanced level.

The stories are not intended to teach new material to the learners, although they may encounter new words and unfamiliar grammatical structures. The purpose is to stimulate speaking practice, and to provide reading and listening practice. By telling the stories, the students will develop skill at the discourse level, learning to link sentences to each other in a coherent manner, from introductory sentences to the final punch line. Weaving the sentences together in connected speech is an essential skill for successful communication. Storytelling is an effective and enjoyable way to develop this skill.

The collection is used most effectively by working with the stories on a regular basis, from one a day to one a week. By continuing with the storytelling over several days or weeks, the students will have the opportunity to improve their narrative skills. At some point, you may want to model dramatic readings of the stories to encourage the students to use pauses, voice modulations, and gestures to make the storytelling more effective.

**The stories may be used in a variety of ways.** The possibilites are many, but the following list of suggestions may be helpful.

**1. Trading Stories – the basic technique.** Give each student in the class a different story card. Have them read through the story while you circulate to help with comprehension. As the students finish and feel they are ready to tell their story, have them find another student with whom, without looking at the text, they exchange stories. For the first time through, allow them to look at the prompts on the back of the card. When the two students have finished sharing, they split up and find other partners to tell their stories to. This can and should continue several times, until they are telling the stories fluently and confidently.

**There are several variations to this technique and other activities that can be done with the stories**. A few are suggested below.

**2. Chain Stories.** Arrange the students in a circle. An even number of students works best. Give a story to every other student in the circle. The students with the stories tell their stories to the students to their left who do not have stories. Then each person who listened turns to the person on their left and tells that person the story, and so on. This technique works better with students at a higher proficiency level.

**3. Story-A-Day.** Each day one student tells a story to the class.

**4. Dictation.** Dictate a story to the students. This is especially good for practicing the punctuation associated with direct speech.

**5. Direct/Indirect Speech Practice.** Read the direct speech lines from a story and have the students rewrite the direct quotes as indirect, and vice versa.

**6. Write with Prompts.** Have the students look at the prompts page and write the stories following the sequence of prompts. After writing, they can compare their sentences with the original.

**7. Listen and Write.** Read a story to the students and then have them write it out from memory. Then have them compare their sentences with the original.

**8. Act it Out.** Give a story to a group of students (the number of students will depend on the story) and have them perform it for their classmates. It may be necessary to have a narrator as well as actors.

**9. Collecting Stories.** Each student shares a favorite Hodja story with a friend not in the class and asks for a story in return. The student brings this new story back to class and presents it live, recorded, or in written form.

From time to time, students and teachers have asked for more stories, and so **Twenty-six Additional Stories** are available for listening practice on the CD. Like the forty illustrated stories, they may be used in a variety of ways:

- For listening comprehension practice. Play – pause – ask.
- For note-taking and re-telling, writing out, or acting out.
- For dictation using the pause and rewind functions.

# *Who was Nasreddin Hodja?*

These stories are an important part of the folklore of the Turkish people. However, they are not simply made-up folk tales.

Historically, there was, in fact, a person known as Nasreddin Hodja who was born in a small village not far from the city of Eskishehir in west central Turkey. He was reportedly born in 1208 and probaby died around 1284. He was buried in a cemetery in the city of Akshehir, also in west central Turkey.

The name Hodja means teacher in Turkish. Originally it refered to a religious teacher, although nowadays it is often used by students as a title of respect for a teacher at the university level. Nasreddin Hodja was a well-educated teacher in religious schools, but he became famous for his wonderful sense of humor.

Since the 13th century, Hodja's stories have been passed down in Turkish-speaking countries in true folk fashion. In the process over the last eight centuries, it is probable that many stories were created by others and attributed to Hodja. Furthermore, they did not stay with the Turkish people. In fact, the stories of Nasreddin Hodja became favorites in every Muslim country and in many countries influenced by Muslim culture. Whatever their sources, these stories are marvelous examples of Turkish humor, and, more than that, they have universal appeal.

ISBN 978-0-86647-441-2

9 780866 474412 >